What a Vacation!

A Family Play

By Jeffrey B. Fuerst
Illustrated by Frank Sofo

Celebration Press
Pearson Learning Group

Contents

Cast of Characters

Mom

Dad

Ray

Jody

Addy

Benny

Featuring:

The Narrator

With:

Tech #1

Tech #2

Woman in Crowd

Lawyer

The Amusement Park Crowd

We Leave, or Try To

(Simple set with free-standing cardboard form of a station wagon. Interior can be represented by chairs and a table—for the back of the car—stacked with suitcases.)

NARRATOR: Welcome, everyone, to the Cardenas family home! Our play starts here, outside the house. You folks in the audience can't see the house because we didn't have the money to build a full set! Well, trust me—it's a lovely three bedroom, painted light blue with rose-colored trim. The gutters are sagging in front, but nothing's perfect.

Now imagine that the grass has been freshly mowed. It's a hot day in mid-July, and the Cardenas family is about to leave for a vacation.

That kid over there *(pointing)* is Ray. He's 12, and he's trying to get all the bags to fit in the back of the family station wagon. *(Suitcases fall, clatter to stage.)* His dad is busy reading a book, *The Happy Trails Guide to a Problem-Free Vacation*. That's Jody, Ray's 15-year-old sister, looking under the hood of the car. Who am I? The Narrator. Think of me as your tour guide. Since we don't have fancy sets, I'll fill you in on some of the details. But remember, only you can see and hear me.

JODY: The transmission fluid is fine, Dad, but we have to add a quart of oil.

NARRATOR: Jody's a mechanical whiz.

DAD: The book says to check the engine belts next.

JODY: Springy, no fray marks. And I cleaned the carburetor last week.

DAD: Now the tires, Jody. *(He reads from the manual.)* "Thirty-one pounds of air on all four sides ensures a safe and happy ride."

(Jody drops to her knees to check the tires with an air pressure gauge. Another suitcase that Ray is trying to load into the car falls out.)

RAY: Dad, how can I fit all this stuff in the car?

DAD: Look at it like a puzzle, Ray, all the pieces fitting together nicely. Or in this case, suitcases.

RAY: I don't even want to take this vacation.

DAD: We've been over that, Ray.

RAY: I wanted to go rappelling. Just some rope is all I need, not all this stuff.

JODY: *(smiling broadly)* You definitely are repelling, Ray.

RAY: Rappelling is a sport, Jody. A really cool sport. You slide down a mountain cliff, down a rope, like this. *(He demonstrates the technique.)* The best part is you could fall at any time.

NARRATOR: Uh-oh. Bad timing on Ray's part. Here comes his mom, and she heard everything. Moms tend to do that, don't they?

(Mom enters, carrying a cooler.)

MOM: Fall at any time, huh? That's exactly why you're not rappelling on our family vacation. Doing that in your climbing club, where it's safe, is fine. But not out in the wilderness.

RAY: But Mom! Climbers always wear a safety harness, like this. *(He pulls out his bag and shows her his climbing gear.)* Besides, I received the Best Climber award in my climbing club.

JODY: That's true. They call him the King of Climb. Or was it the Duke of Descent? Or maybe—

MOM: I get it, Jody. The point is, I don't want to spend our vacation visiting Ray at the hospital.

DAD: Togetherness, Ray, that's the theme of the Cardenas family vacation.

JODY: Oh, no. Here it comes.

DAD: A family is a team, guys, a unit. A well-oiled machine.

JODY: *(muttering)* We don't even eat dinner together very often anymore.

MOM: We don't even eat dinner together very often anymore.

RAY: *(muttering)* And don't even get me started about the weekends.

DAD: And don't even get me started about the weekends.

RAY: Hey, we're busy kids. We've got lots of things we have to do.

MOM: We understand that you're busy, Ray, but between soccer practice and basketball games and piano lessons, not to mention climbing club, we never get to see much of you.

RAY: I'll give up piano lessons if you want to see more of me.

MOM: Nice try, but I don't think so. Jody's also busy with dance class or chess club or babysitting, along with her "how-to" books and magazines on car repair.

RAY: *(teasingly, to Jody)* Or going to the mall.

MOM: And between all that, Dad and I have to get Addy off to preschool, then to swimming or to her after-school program.

(Addy enters, carrying a bucket of sand toys.)

ADDY: Here I am!

NARRATOR: That's Addy, the youngest member of the Cardenas family. She'll be four-and-a-half years old next month.

MOM: Do you have everything you want to bring?

ADDY: Yes.

DAD: Did you visit the bathroom?

ADDY: Yes.

MOM: Anyway, vacation is the only chance we really have to be together as a family.

DAD: And you know what they say, guys. A family that plays together . . . .

JODY: Oh, Dad.

DAD: *(holding up his book)* It says so right here. It also says, "Be a team." That's why Jody is helping me get the car ready.

MOM: And Addy is helping me close up the house. Let's go back inside and double-check the stove, Addy.

(She walks swiftly offstage into the house. Addy follows.)

RAY: *(grumbling)* And the well-known team of Me, Myself, and I is loading the car.

(Mom and Addy return.)

MOM: Stove's off. Anything else? The water!

(Mom and Addy run back into the house quickly and then return almost immediately.)

MOM: Water's off. Hmm. Did I put the light on the timer?

(Mom and Addy run back into the house and then return.)

MOM: Timer's on. House is checked and ready.

RAY: And that's the last bag. Suitcases are loaded.

JODY: The car is ready, too.

DAD: Then it's time to hit the road!

ADDY: Wait! I forgot something!

MOM: What is it, Addy?

ADDY: I don't have Benny; we can't leave without him. *(starts to cry)*

MOM: You forgot to pack your teddy?

ADDY: I think so. Maybe. Maybe he's still in the house, all alone, or maybe he's lost.

DAD: *(consoling Addy)* Ray, check the bags.

RAY: Oh, brother! *(He begins to take out and unpack all the bags.)*

MOM: Come on, Addy. We'll go back in the house to look for Benny.

RAY: Don't you think we're going backwards instead of forward here?

DAD: These are just the little potholes of a family vacation. We'll laugh about them later, guys. Trust me!

RAY: *(mumbling under his breath as he struggles with a suitcase)* Some vacation.

NARRATOR: End of scene.

(The Narrator can control the lights or cue the lighting person to turn off the classroom lights.)

Getting There Is NOT Half the Fun

(Interior of station wagon can be represented by chairs. Painted backdrop of a country road through rolling hills.)

NARRATOR: It's now a few hours later. Dad is driving along a quiet country road through rolling hills. Look—a dairy farm. Imagine that those chairs they're sitting on are really the seats of the station wagon.

(Addy, clutching her teddy bear, sits in the middle of the back seat, between Ray, who is playing a hand-held video game, and Jody, who is reading a magazine.)

DAD: Kids, did you know that this road was once part of the Underground Railroad? Slaves used it to escape to the North before the Civil War.

RAY: *(rolling his eyes)* That's great, Dad.

DAD: It wasn't really a railroad, you know, but—

JODY: Ray, close your window, please. My hair is blowing all over the place.

ADDY: Mom, Ray is bothering me.

RAY: *(looking up, surprised)* I didn't do anything!

ADDY: You pushed me.

RAY: I didn't touch you.

DAD: *(gently scolding, not really angry)* Kids! You don't want me to have to stop the car, do you?

(silence)

ADDY: Are we there yet?

DAD: Not yet.

(silence)

ADDY: How much longer?

DAD: A while.

(silence)

ADDY: How much longer now?

DAD: *(frustrated)* A while minus five seconds!

MOM: Let's sing a song to pass the time. "Row, row, row your boat . . . ." C'mon everybody, in a round, "Row, row, row your boat gently down the stream."

ADDY, RAY, JODY: "Row, row, row your boat."

ADDY: Ray and Jody are singing on my turn.

RAY: I go next.

ADDY: No, I go next. I'm the youngest.

JODY: No, I go next. I'm the oldest.

MOM: All right, let's sing a different song.
(Each child sings a different song at the same time. The Narrator covers his or her ears from the racket.)

ADDY: "Twinkle, twinkle, little star. . . ."
RAY: *(rolling his eyes)* "The wheels on the car go round and round . . . ."
JODY: "She loves you, yeah, yeah, yeah . . . ."
MOM: I meant we should all sing the same song!
(silence)
ADDY: Are we there yet now?
MOM: How about if we play a car game?
JODY: How about Twenty Questions?
ADDY: Uh-oh, I don't think Benny feels too good.
DAD: How do you play that?
(Mom looks at Addy, who has a hand over her mouth.)
RAY: I don't think that's a game, Dad.
NARRATOR: End of scene. Oh well, at least they're *finally* on vacation.

There's a Scenic View Around Here Somewhere

(Outdoor rustic scene on painted backdrop with high waterfall flowing into a gorge at one end.)

NARRATOR: It's now a few hours later on the same day. You'll be relieved to know that the family is taking a break from the long car ride. They're hiking up a rocky trail to this clearing. Here they come now.

(Enter family. Dad stumbles around while peering through binoculars. Mom is reading a map; Ray is lugging a camera and tripod.)

JODY: I can't walk another step.

ADDY: My feet hurt!

RAY: Yeah, Dad, where is this scenic view?

DAD: It's around here somewhere.

MOM: According to the map . . . .

DAD: I don't need a map.

I have an internal compass.

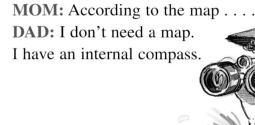

RAY: Is that what you call it?

JODY: Cool! Look.

(Jody scoots to the other side of the stage, by the waterfall, and peers offstage. The rest of the family follows her.)

DAD: *(pointing offstage, where Jody is looking)* There, Cardenas family, is your scenic view.

RAY: A waterfall? You made us hike up a mountain to look at a waterfall?

DAD: No, we hiked up a mountain to take a scenic family photo! Don't move until I set up the tripod. *(fumbles around with his camera equipment)*

RAY: So, why do you think they call it a waterfall anyway? *(pretends to slip and fall)*

MOM: Ray, dear, that's really not very funny.

ADDY: All this water is making me thirsty.

NARRATOR: *(loudly)* Have you ever seen such a beautiful waterfall? Tons of water rushing over the cliff and pounding the ground below. BA-BOOM! It's so loud I can barely hear myself think. *(reverts to his regular voice)* Oh, time for yet another family photo!

(Dad scurries back to family for the photo.)

JODY: Dad, you forgot the lens cap.

DAD: Oh, yeah.

(Dad runs back to the tripod, puts down the remote shutter release, removes the lens cap from the camera, and then runs back to be in the picture.)

JODY: I hope Dad's not going to make us pose for a picture every 30 seconds.

MOM: Of course he is, but I brought the other camera—the one that takes instant pictures. That should save us some time.

DAD: Okay, everyone, say "cheese!"

ALL: Cheese.

JODY: Dad, you forgot the remote shutter release.

DAD: Oh, right.

(Dad runs back, gets the remote shutter release, and returns.)

DAD: One more time, gang. Say "cheese."

ALL: Cheese.

(Dad clicks the camera, but nothing happens.)

DAD: Hmm, what's wrong with this thing?

JODY: Did you change the batteries?

(Dad runs back to the camera one more time, puts in batteries, and then returns to be in the picture.)

ADDY: Can I stop smiling? My face hurts.

RAY: It's killing me, yuck-yuck.

ADDY: Mom!

DAD: Once more, everyone! Say "family vacation!"

ALL: Cheese.

ADDY: I like orange cheese.

(Dad clicks the remote shutter release.)

RAY: All this talk about cheese is making me hungry.

MOM: I think we could use a snack break.

(Mom hands out crackers from her bag. Addy refuses to take any.)

ADDY: I only like orange crackers.

(Dad takes the camera off the tripod and positions himself carefully on the ground to take an "artistic" shot of Addy.)

DAD: Let me take one more picture of you, Addy. Watch the birdie!

ADDY: I don't see any birds.

DAD: That's just an expression. It goes back to the early days of photography when—

ADDY: But I do see a kitty cat.

DAD: There are no cats in these woods, honey.

(A skunk could be represented by a child dressed up like a skunk crawling onto the stage. Or, a stuffed toy skunk can be tossed onto the stage from the wings.)

ADDY: He's a black kitty.

DAD: Black?

ADDY: With a long white stripe on his back.

DAD: A white stripe?

MOM: Skunk!

RAY, JODY, ADDY: Skunk! Skunk! Skunk!

NARRATOR: Skunk! Pee-yew.

(Everyone scatters offstage except for Dad, who runs back, grabs the camera and tripod, and follows them.)

DAD: This should make a great family photo!

NARRATOR: *(returns from offstage, holding his nose)* End of scene. So far, you might say this vacation stinks.

On the Shores of
Lake Brackish

(The set is the interior of a very rustic cabin. A table and chairs are set in front of a painted backdrop.)

NARRATOR: It's a few hours later, and things are starting to smell a lot better. Dusk is settling over a cabin in the woods. Can't you hear the birds and crickets? *(pause)* TWEET-TWEET. CHIRP-CHIRP. Anyhow, here comes the Cardenas family.

DAD: Here we are. Cabin 17! This is going to be our home away from home.

RAY: There's no television!

JODY: Or refrigerator!

MOM: Honey, where's the bathroom?

DAD: There isn't one!

(Silence as they all look at Dad)

DAD: There's no television, no VCR, no stereo or radio, and no phone. No fridge, stove, toaster oven, or microwave. In fact, there's no electricity and no running water. I thought it would be fun to rough it. We can live as people did in the 1800s.

MOM: You told me it would be rustic, but I didn't think you meant archaic.

RAY: Yeah, Dad, this is prehistoric.

DAD: Come on, guys! What's happened to your sense of adventure?

RAY: I think it ran away with the skunk.

DAD: This is going to be great! We don't need all the trappings of the modern world to have fun.

JODY: I think people built all those trappings for a reason.

DAD: Nonsense! There's a lot we can do here; just think about it.

MOM: I guess you're right—as long as we do it together, as a family . . . .

RAY: Like what?

DAD: Well, how about we start with a nature walk.

(Dad consults a nature guidebook while Mom pulls various items out of a suitcase.)

MOM: If we're going on a nature walk, then everyone needs to put on bug repellent and sunscreen.

DAD: This is going to be fun! We can pick and eat wild berries.

MOM: Only if we identify them carefully and wash them first.

JODY: Can we go swimming instead?

DAD: Sure. We're vacationing on the shores of a real man-made lake.

RAY: A man-made lake? That sounds pretty modern. Was it here in the 1800s?

MOM: *(pulling out items as she names them.)* I've got bathing suits, goggles, earplugs, nose clips, and bathing caps.

JODY: Earplugs?

MOM: And we need to be sure to wear these flip-flops on our feet, because the bottom of the lake might be mucky.

JODY: On second thought, I'm not going any place where things squish between my toes.

RAY: *(sighing)* How about boating?

MOM: Just make sure you wear a life jacket.

ADDY: I don't like boats.

DAD: I saw a volleyball net on the campgrounds.

ADDY: Benny loves volleyball.

RAY: I'll play.

JODY: If everybody else wants to . . . .

MOM: It's settled then; our first vacation activity will be volleyball. Here's sunscreen, sunglasses, sun hats, and put some of this white stuff on your nose.

RAY: It's cloudy out!

MOM: All the more reason to protect yourself against those sneaky ultraviolet rays.

(Lights flicker on and off.)

NARRATOR: Whoops! See those flickering lights? That means we have to pretend we're in the middle of a lightning storm. BOOM! BOOM! That's thunder. I don't know how to make the sound, but rain has begun pouring down in torrents on the cabin.

JODY: So volleyball is out.

RAY: *(sarcastically)* Anyone interested in a round of charades?

ADDY: *(looking out a window)* Mom, did you pack my raincoat?

(Mom starts to repack all the stuff she's hauled out of the suitcases.)

MOM: What a vacation this is turning out to be— and no bathroom!

NARRATOR *(putting on a rain hat)* Very wet end of scene.

An Outbreak of Cabin Fever

(Same interior scene. Various pots, cups, and buckets are placed on the cabin floor to catch the water leaking heavily through the roof.)

NARRATOR: *(sneezes)* I think I'm catching a cold. It is now five days later, and it's still raining. None of the Cardenas family members are talking much to one another. *(Jody listens to music through her headphones; Ray plays with his video game; Dad leafs through travel brochures.)* Here come Mom and Addy, back from washing the family's clothes at the campground's laundromat.

ADDY: *(singing happily)* "It's raining, it's pouring."

RAY: We noticed.

DAD: *(empties one of the buckets that catches water leaking through the roof)* Well, Jody should be happy. We've got plenty of running water! *(indicates the leaks, jokingly)*

RAY: A few more days of this and we'll need to build an ark to get home.

MOM: Look at the bright side. *(Everyone turns to hear what she has to say.)* With all this rain, no one's getting sunburned!

JODY: This disaster wouldn't have happened if we had gone to Club Fun'n'Sun, the way I wanted to.

RAY: No way! We should have gone to Really Cool Adventures Theme Park, where I wanted to go. They have an awesome indoor rock-climbing wall.

JODY: Not the rock-climbing thing again. I thought you were going to give that a rest.

RAY: *(muttering)* It would be better than spending a week at Club Fun'n'Sun.

DAD: Who's up for trying to visit another local tourist attraction? I've been looking through these brochures. Let's choose a site that seems promising.

JODY: The tourist places around here are so tacky—a house made out of old tires, the Museum of Potatoes That Look Like Celebrities.

MOM: Maybe it's just me, but all the potatoes in that museum seemed to look like Elvis Presley—in his later period.

JODY: And that tour of the olive grove was the pits. No pun intended.

DAD: *(rifles through the brochures once again)*
There's the Knock-Hockey Hall of Fame and the
Driftwood Antique Furniture Outlet. How about a
trip to this hydroelectric plant? It has the world's
fifth largest electromagnet!

JODY: Oh, now that's an attraction.

DAD: That's enough, Jody. No one's happy with the
rain, but we have to make the best of it. Just because
we're on vacation doesn't mean I can't ground you.

JODY: Ground me? This whole vacation is like
being grounded. *(glares at everyone and then clamps
on her headset and pouts)* What a vacation this is
turning out to be!

ADDY: May I have two more quarters, Mommy?

MOM: What for?

ADDY: So I can go back to the laundromat and watch the clothes spin in the dryer again.

MOM: I've already told you, honey, that we'll do only one load a day.

ADDY: But Benny and I really want to go and watch the laundry!

MOM and DAD: Sigh!

NARRATOR: End of scene. *(shakes head)* Sounds as if this vacation is a washout. Get it? Washout?

Ride of a Lifetime

(Scene on backdrop is a large outline of a Ferris wheel. Benches or chairs up on a platform represent the car the characters will ride inside. Carnival-goers randomly walk by.)

NARRATOR: It's the next day. The good news is that the sun has come out, and the Cardenas family has decided to go to an amusement park. The bad news is that every other family in a 100-mile radius has decided to go to the same place. *(Narrator mimes getting jostled by large crowds of people.)* There are rides, refreshment stands, carnival games, souvenirs—and, of course, lines. I'll take one of those. *(Narrator mimes paying a vendor and then puts on a glow-in-the-dark headband or some other silly souvenir.)*

ADDY: *(excited)* Wow! I love Gameland!

JODY: *(looking around, disappointed)* The lines are already so long!

RAY: At least we made it—even if it is the last day of our vacation.

DAD: *(annoyed, carrying camera on tripod)* I can't believe what they charged us for parking!

MOM: It is pricier than I thought. But at least the kids aren't fighting. That makes it worth it.

DAD: And we are all together.

JODY: *(embarrassed)* I can't believe you made us all wear the same kind of T-shirt.

NARRATOR: *(holding up, or putting on, a T-shirt)* It's a bright yellow T-shirt that has a group photo of the Cardenas family printed on it with these words: "Cardenas Family Fun Fest."

DAD: What do you want to do first?

ADDY: I want a Gameland teddy bear for Benny.

DAD: We'll look at those later.

RAY: Let's try the Brain Imploder ride!

JODY: I like the bumper cars.

RAY: But the Brain Imploder is a superfast roller coaster that goes upside down and inside out.

JODY: Boring. You have no control.

RAY: That's the point.

JODY: Bumper cars are more fun.

DAD: Anyone for the "What's-a-Matter Horn"?

RAY: Brain Imploder!

JODY: Bumper cars!

RAY: Brain Imploder!

JODY: Bumper cars!

ADDY: Can we get my new teddy bear now?

MOM: I thought we were here on a family vacation. Let's try to do something all together. Who wants to ride the Ferris wheel?

RAY: Now that's boring.

JODY: No, thanks.

ADDY: Ferris what?

DAD: Well, dear, it's really not my first choice either.

MOM: Then we're all agreed. We're going on the Ferris wheel!

(They wind their way through the crowds to the Ferris wheel.)

NARRATOR: Now this scene in the play can't work unless you do your part, audience. See these benches? You have to imagine this is a car on an old-fashioned Ferris wheel. Here comes the Cardenas family to take their seats. Now imagine that they are riding to the top. *(pause)* There they go!

MOM: *(looking out through binoculars)* What a fantastic view. You can see for miles!

DAD: Did you know that this Ferris wheel is built like the very first Ferris wheel, which made its debut at the 1893 Chicago World's Fair? It is 264 feet high!

RAY: Dad, where do you get this stuff?

DAD: Right here, in my trusty guidebook.

JODY: This ride is not good for my hair. I should have worn a headband.

ADDY: *(clutching Benny)* Mom, make Ray stop bothering me.

RAY: I didn't do anything.

ADDY: You poked me.

RAY: I didn't touch you.

ADDY: Ray, you're on my side.

RAY: I am not on your side! There is no side!

DAD: Kids, kids! You don't want me to stop this ride, do you?

NARRATOR: SCREEECH! Yikes! That's the sound of the Ferris wheel machinery grinding very quickly to a halt.

(The Cardenas family members lurch forward in their seats as the Ferris wheel suddenly stops. They look around, surprised.)

JODY: Cool trick, Dad!

DAD: Huh?

TECH #1: *(yelling "up" to the family sitting in the Ferris wheel car)* Attention, Ferris wheel riders! We apologize for the inconvenience, but we are experiencing mechanical difficulties!

JODY: Now what?

MOM: We could sing a song.

(Everyone stares at her.) Play a game?

DAD: Now's the time for a fun family photo.

(He pulls out the instant camera.)

RAY, JODY, ADDY: Not again!

DAD: Okay, everyone!

RAY, JODY, ADDY: *(in a monotone)* We know, Dad. "Cheese."

(Dad clicks the camera, and out spits a photo.)

NARRATOR: SPROING! Uh-oh! The Ferris wheel just dropped a couple of feet. BROING! Fasten your seat belts. SPROING! It's turning into a bumpy ride.

(Benny slips out of Addy's hands.)

ADDY: Oops!

DAD: Whoa!

JODY: Eek!

MOM: Oh, my.

RAY: Awesome!

TECH #1: Okay, folks. We'll get you down.

NARRATOR: SPROING! ZUMM! SPROING! ZUMM! The Ferris wheel seems to be acting up.

(The family jolts forward with some screaming.)

BANG! The Ferris wheel car with the Cardenases in it has returned to the bottom. Whew! My stomach is doing flip-flops just from watching.

(Everyone but Ray exits the car holding his or her head or stomach and groaning. Ray emerges energized.)

RAY: Let's do it again!

TECH #1: Sorry, but this ride is closed until further notice.

RAY: Bummer.

DAD: I don't know about the rest of you, but I could use a cold glass of lemonade.

RAY: Then on to the Brain Imploder!

JODY: Boring.

MOM: I think I'm a little dizzy.

DAD: Let me help you.

NARRATOR: The Cardenas family heads to a refreshment stand offstage. Wait! What's Addy doing? She's running back to the Ferris wheel.

ADDY: Don't worry, Benny. I didn't forget you.

NARRATOR: She's getting into the Ferris wheel car and searching under the seats for her teddy bear. She is out of the technicians' view.

TECH #1: I think the problem is with the turn cogs.

TECH #2: I think the axle might be cracked.

TECH #1: There's only one way to find out.

NARRATOR: Oh, no! The technician is pushing the start lever!

NARRATOR: BROING! The Ferris wheel is slowly starting up.

ADDY: *(hidden beneath the seats)* Hey!

TECH #2: What was that?

TECH #1: This brake lever needs oiling.

ADDY: Hey! Stop!

TECH #1: It's stiff. Give me a hand.

(Tech #2 helps him push the lever. It snaps off.)

TECH #1: Now it needs soldering.

TECH #2: Better put up the signs.

(Tech #2 puts up "CLOSED FOR REPAIRS" and "DO NOT ENTER" signs. The technicians go for tools.)

NARRATOR: BROING! Yikes! The Ferris wheel is moving upward—with Addy in it. BROING! It's not stopping! BROING! BROING! SCRE-E-ECH! Now it's stopped—at the very top.

(Addy stands up.)

ADDY: *(looking scared)* Hey! What happened?

WOMAN IN CROWD: Look! At the top of the Ferris wheel. There's a little girl in a yellow T-shirt.

ADDY: *(clutching Benny)* Help! Somebody! We're up here!

NARRATOR: Here come Mom, Dad, Ray, and Jody pushing through the crowd, looking for Addy. They can't hear or see her at the top of the Ferris wheel.

DAD: Addy, Addy!

RAY: Addy!

JODY: Addy!

MOM: I thought Addy was with you, dear! Addy!

WOMAN IN CROWD: *(spotting the Cardenas family calling)* The same yellow T-shirts! *(darts through the crowd and taps Mom on the shoulder)* Are you looking for a little girl?

MOM: Yes!

WOMAN: I think she's stuck on the Ferris wheel!

MOM: The Ferris wheel?

(They follow the woman back to the Ferris wheel.)

MOM: Addy!

ADDY: *(petrified)* Mommy!

DAD: Oh, Addy!

ADDY: Daddy! Help! Benny and I want to come down now!

DAD: We'll get you down in a jiffy, honey. Don't be scared. *(hurriedly to Mom, Jody, Ray)* Okay, guys, think!

ADDY: It'll be okay, Benny. Don't be scared.

JODY: Let me find out what's wrong.

(Jody runs to where the technicians disappeared.)

MOM: Sit tight, Addy!

DAD: *(peering up at Addy with the binoculars)* She'll be okay; she's a trouper.

MOM: She doesn't like heights.

RAY: I wish I were stuck up there. I love heights.

MOM: That's right. You do.

(Mom suddenly calms down and sizes up Ray.)

NARRATOR: Hmmm. I know what it means when Mom gets that look in her eyes. She's cooking up a plan.

(Jody returns, out of breath, followed by Tech #1 and Tech #2.)

JODY: Here's the deal. It's not terrible.

DAD: That's a relief.

JODY: But it's not good.

DAD: That's not such a relief.

TECH #1: The lever that controls the brake is broken.

JODY: *(picking up the camera tripod)* But I think I can fix that.

NARRATOR: SPROING! I know that sound. The Ferris wheel car that Addy is in has slipped another three feet. Cover your eyes!

MOM: Addy!

DAD: Take it easy, dear. That old-style Ferris wheel car is enclosed with wire mesh. It's impossible to fall out.

JODY: The bigger problem is that the axle may be cracked.

TECH #1: We won't know until we take a look.

TECH #2: We can't get up there until we get a bucket truck here, and that may take a while.

NARRATOR: BROING! Ohh! I knew I should have stayed home today.

ADDY: Hold on, Benny! Daddy!

(A crowd gathers.)

TECH #1: We may have to make some repairs before we bring the car down.

MOM: Where do the repairs need to be made?

TECH #2: In the center of the wheel, where the axle is.

MOM: How high is that?

DAD: This Ferris wheel is 264 feet high, so the center of the wheel should be half that—132 feet.

MOM: *(turning to Ray)* How good are you, Ray?

RAY: Mom?

MOM: Can you do it?

RAY: Do what?

MOM: Climb, Ray, climb!

RAY: Me? You want me to climb? But you said you hated the idea of me climbing, except in class.

MOM: This is an emergency.

DAD: And you are the King of Climb, the Duke of Descent.

RAY: I don't know. *(walking toward wheel)* I could give it a try. It's not exactly what I'm used to, but I'm sure I could do it.

MOM: Is there a rock-climbing wall in this place?

DAD: *(checking the map)* Yes! It's in the next section.

MOM: Fantastic. Ray, see if you can borrow their climbing rope and safety harness.

TECH #1: I'll get it.

(He dashes through the crowd.)

MOM: Ray, here's Dad's instant camera. See if you can take a picture of the axle and then drop the picture back down to us.

TECH #2: We'll be able to troubleshoot from here.

JODY: Mom, you're a genius!

(Jody and Tech #2 head toward the Ferris wheel's broken brake lever. Tech #1 returns with the safety harness, which Ray straps on.)

TECH #1: *(handing Ray a bike helmet)* Wear this; it will help protect you.

MOM: *(to Ray)* I shouldn't be letting you do this.

RAY: Don't worry, Mom. It'll be just like climbing with my club back home.

DAD: Ray is our best chance.

RAY: And Addy needs me.

DAD: I'll throw the rope over that supporting brace up there, hold it myself, and feed you the line. Good luck, son.

RAY: No problem, Dad.

(They hug quickly as Ray darts off. Dad anchors rope. Ray mimes climbing the spokes of the wheel.)

CROWD: Go, Ray, go!

(A lawyer wearing a business suit and tie and carrying a briefcase runs up from the audience and hands the Narrator a formal-looking letter, which he opens and reads.)

NARRATOR: Oh, right. *(to audience)* The publisher of this play wants to remind all members of the audience that the actions depicted herein are for entertainment purposes only. They should not be interpreted as an endorsement to climb Ferris wheels or any other structures that children may actually encounter at a real amusement park.

LAWYER: Thank you. *(He walks off.)*

NARRATOR: Now back to the play. BROING! That old Ferris wheel is acting up—or should I say down?—again. Yikes!

(Ray briefly loses his footing but resumes climbing.)

CROWD: Ohh! Ahh!

RAY: That was close.

MOM: Be careful, Ray!

DAD: We'll get through this—as a family.

TECH #1: Let's get to work on that brake.

JODY: See if you can operate the STOP mechanism with one of the legs of the tripod. We'll use it to replace the broken lever.

TECH #1: One leg isn't strong enough.

JODY: Try binding all three together for extra strength.

RAY: I made it!

CROWD: Yay, Ray! Way to go!

(The crowd claps and shouts encouragement as Ray snaps the photo of the axle.)

RAY: *(tossing photo)* Here comes the photo!

(Dad retrieves photo and brings it to the techs and Jody.)

DAD: Great job, son!

TECH #2: *(fiddling with the camera tripod)* Perfect! All three legs of the tripod put together will be strong enough to replace the broken lever. Let's just push them into place.

TECH #1: Push.

DAD: Let me help. One, two, three—

NARRATOR: GR-R-UNCHH. Together they move the tripod lever back and forth and SPROING!— the Ferris wheel drops another three feet!

CROWD: Ohh! Ahh!

RAY: Whoa!

MOM: Ray!

ADDY: *(terrified)* Mommy!

MOM: Addy!

RAY: *(climbing again)* It's okay, Addy. I'm coming.

ADDY: *(to Ray)* Ray! What are you doing?

RAY: Coming to rescue you.

ADDY: You climbed all the way up here?

RAY: Yeah, squirt. Do you care where I sit?

ADDY: You can sit on my side, Ray.

TECH #1: *(examining the photo)* It's not the axle!

TECH #2: But the cogs look as if they might slip again.

JODY: Is it safe to bring them down?

TECH #2: I think so. The brake is powerful.

TECH #1: We'll move it down slowly and carefully.

NARRATOR: ZUMMMMM! The Ferris wheel is moving smoothly now. Whew! Here comes the car with Addy and Ray.

CROWD: Yahoo! All right!

NARRATOR: ZUMM! WHOOSH! The car is safely at the bottom!

(He begins to clap, as does the crowd.)

(Ray helps Addy out. They're immediately hugged by Jody. Mom and Dad then hug them all.)

MOM: Ray! Jody! Addy!

DAD: Thank goodness you're all safe and sound. You were very brave, Addy. Nice work, Ray. Fast thinking, Jody.

JODY: We couldn't have done it without you.

RAY: Or Mom.

ADDY: Wait! Wait!

DAD: What's wrong now?

ADDY: I forgot Benny!

(She skips toward the Ferris wheel car.)

ADDY: He'll be scared on the Ferris wheel all alone without me.

NARRATOR: End of scene. After all that excitement, I could use a vacation!

What a Vacation!

(Interior scene of station wagon can be represented by chairs. Painted backdrop of a country road bathed in the brilliant colors of a spectacular sunset.)

NARRATOR: It is the next day. The Cardenas family is back in the old station wagon on their way home.

ALL: *(singing in unison and laughing)* "On top of spaghetti, all covered with cheese; I lost my poor meatball, when somebody sneezed."

MOM: That was great, kids! Who picks the next song?

RAY: Why don't we let Jody choose, because she's the oldest.

JODY: Thanks. Of course I'm the oldest, but I think that Ray should pick the next song because he's the bravest of all.

RAY: Who am I to argue with that? *(He begins to sing and the others join in.)* "The Ferris wheel goes round and round."

ALL: "Round and round, round and round. The Ferris wheel goes round and round."

DAD: *(singing in off-key voice)* "Unless you're on the Ferris wheel at Gameland!"

ALL: *(laughter)*

DAD: *(chuckling)* I've been driving for over an hour. How come nobody has asked me, "Are we there yet?"

RAY: Maybe we don't want the vacation to be over this soon.

DAD: Just because the vacation is over doesn't mean the fun is over.

JODY: *(looking through a stack of photos and giggling)* I hate to admit it, Dad, but some of the photos you took—

RAY: And took and took—

JODY: Are hilarious!

ADDY: Let me see!

DAD: Find the picture I took of Addy near the waterfall. That's a good one.

ADDY: Yeah, and here's a picture of me holding Benny up high.

RAY: Here are some pictures of us playing charades. Jody, you look funny when you're trying to think hard.

JODY: Those are a laugh and a half. Look at this one of Mom.

RAY: Mom, what were you trying to show when you stuck your fingers in your ears?

MOM: *(looking at the photo, then demonstrating)* Oh, that one. I was a satellite dish.

RAY: Cute, Mom!

ADDY: I hope it rains for a week when we get home, so we can play again.

JODY: I'm in, even if it doesn't rain.

RAY: Here's one of us trying to swim at the lake. Addy's wearing her flip-flops.

MOM: The mosquitoes were the size of tennis balls.

JODY: This was the best vacation ever.

MOM: Even the Ferris wheel?

ADDY: That was the best part. They gave me a bunch of Gameland teddy bears.

RAY: And a bunch of guest passes so we can go back next year.

DAD: With free parking!

(Everyone laughs.)

MOM: I know a way to make the time not pass by so quickly. *(She starts to sing "Row, row, row your boat," followed by everyone else, in a perfect round. The singing ends so that we hear each person singing the last line of the song individually.)*

MOM: "Life is but a dream."

DAD: "Life is but a dream."

JODY: "Life is but a dream."

RAY: "Life is but a dream."

ADDY: "Life is but a dream."

(They give each other a round of applause.)

NARRATOR: What a vacation it turned out to be after all! End of our family play. You can clap now.